WHILE THERE IS

Tea

THERE IS
HOPE

Published by Collins
An imprint of HarperCollins Publishers
Robroyston Gate,
Glasgow G33 IJN

HarperCollins Publishers
Macken House, 39/40 Mayor Street Upper,
Dublin I, D0I C9W8, Ireland

Published in partnership with Imperial War Museums
Lambeth Road,
London SEI 6HZ
www.iwm.org.uk

First edition 2025
© HarperCollins Publishers 2025
Text © Alex Johnson 2025

A catalogue record for this book is available from the British Library.

ISBN 978-0-00-874400-7

I0 9 8 7 6 5 4 3 2 I

If you would like to comment on any aspect of this publication, please contact
the Publishers at the above address or online.
e-mail: collins.reference@harpercollins.co.uk

Printed in Europe

MIX
Paper | Supporting
responsible forestry
FSC™ C007454
www.fsc.org

This book contains FSC™ certified paper and other controlled
sources to ensure responsible forest management.

For more information visit: www.harpercollins.co.uk/green

WHILE THERE IS

Tea

THERE IS

HOPE

ALEX JOHNSON

CONTENTS

INTRODUCTION

On the morning of the Battle of Waterloo, June 18, 1815, the Duke of Wellington stopped at a cottage very close to the front line. It had been raining heavily and the men of the 95th Rifles were brewing tea to perk themselves up. The duke was offered a cup of hot, sweet tea, which he accepted before riding off for a date with destiny.

Tea provided something special to Britain's armed forces, who benefitted from its warmth and invigorating properties from the days of the Napoleonic Wars onwards, during conflicts in the Crimea, the Boer War, and, especially, the First World War.

By the 1930s, Britain as a nation had been drinking tea for at least 300 years and it had become the staple drink of choice for workers, soldiers and aristocrats alike. Tea room numbers blossomed in the interwar years, and tea historian William Ukers wrote in his encyclopaedic 1935 book *All About Tea*: "If he is to be happy, the Briton must have his tea – and good tea – whenever he wants it."

When Prime Minister Neville Chamberlain declared war on Germany on September 3, 1939, Britain was drinking about 10lb of tea per person a year, roughly five cups a day. In the words of novelist George Orwell, who joined the Home Guard in 1940, tea was simply "one of the mainstays of civilisation in this country".

But war threatened to ruin the daily cuppa(s): when the SS Gairsoppa was sunk by a German U-Boat in February 1941, it was carrying 1,765 tons of tea, sufficient to keep two thirds of Britain's caddies stocked for an entire week.

Nevertheless, throughout the war, tea drinking developed into a symbol of the British at their best: unruffled, unmoved, and unflappable, whether on the home front or the front line. Side by side, people did their bit, drank tea, and got on with the matter in hand. The archives of the Imperial War Museum are overflowing with photographs of members of the armed forces sipping tea together all over the world, and images of those back at home getting on fine despite their much-reduced weekly ration.

There was barely an aspect of life that tea did not enrich. A cup of tea with friends reinforced community spirit, gave workers in factories, mines, and on farms a welcome break, and offered comfort to those who had lost their homes or loved ones in bombing raids.

The power of a cup of tea is as evident today as it was back then. The belief that tea brings people together has been reinforced by recent studies indicating that tea consumption rose significantly during the coronavirus pandemic.

Whatever troubles life throws at us, we still love our tea.

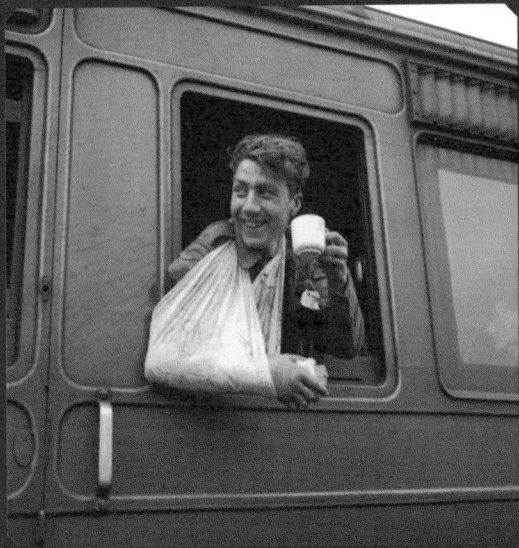

NONE FOR THE POT

As a major importer of food, Britain knew its supply lines would be vulnerable to attack during war, so in the run-up to the Second World War the Ministry of Food developed plans for dealing with potential shortages. By summer 1939, millions of ration books had already been printed. Since tea had been rationed in 1918 it was hardly a surprise when its regulation returned, though that did not happen until the summer of 1940 when it joined "basic foods" – such as cheese, butter, sugar and bacon – and petrol.

A series of leaflets called *Food Facts* was regularly published by the Ministry of Food to offer advice on cooking with these restrictions, including the repeated guidance that people should add a spoonful of tea for each person but "none for the pot". More advice was forthcoming in the following years – a public information film called *Tea Making Tips,* produced by the Empire Tea Bureau trade association in 1941, reminded viewers never to store tea next to disinfectant or cheese since this would affect its flavour (and not in a good way).

In addition, the government did its best to safeguard the country's stocks of tea, buying up as much as it could as soon as war broke out, and dispersing it to hundreds of warehouses around the country to prevent German bombers wreaking a tea catastrophe on London. Mincing Lane, the hub of the tea trade in the capital, was indeed badly bombed in May 1941.

Estimates suggest that, in terms of weight, the government bought more tea than artillery shells and explosives, and only slightly less than bullets.

The result of all these precautions was that tea drinkers over the tender age of 5 had to make do with 2oz per person a week, rising to 3oz for the over-70s towards the end of the war. This worked out at two or three cups of not very strong tea a day, though extra rations were available to the forces and those in key occupations, such as steelworkers. Rationing also affected shops – in its teahouses, Lyons decided to make 100 cups to the pound instead of the 85 of pre-1939.

While hot, sweet tea was the most common way of enjoying a cuppa, rationing didn't bother everyone. In his essay *A Nice Cup of Tea* for the *Evening Standard* in January 1946, George Orwell included comprehensive instructions on making the perfect cup of tea in which he controversially argued that it should be drunk without sugar, which simply swamped the taste with sweetness.

Tea came off the ration in October 1952, with newspaper headlines and celebrations marking the happy occasion for millions of tea drinkers across Britain.

Laid out here is the 1942 weekly ration (and ration book) for a
Mr Norman Franklin: tea, egg, cheese, butter, sugar, bacon, and lard.
Everybody tried to make it go further, from supplementing dried
egg with cornflour to adding a saccharine tablet to the teapot to
sweeten the whole brew rather than one cup.

MUFFINS

14oz plain flour
2½ level teaspoons salt
¾oz yeast or dried yeast
1 rounded teaspoon sugar
½ pint lukewarm water

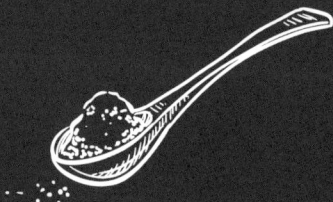

Sieve the flour and salt together into a basin. Blend the yeast
with the sugar, and stir slowly as you pour in the lukewarm water.
Add this to the flour, and mix to a smooth dough. Continue to stir
the dough with a wooden spoon for 5 minutes. Cover the basin with
a cloth and leave it in a warm place for ¾ hour for the dough to rise.

Knock back the dough to its original size. Cover again with the
cloth and leave in a warm place for a ¼ hour to rise again. Divide
the dough into six portions, mould into rounds, and fit into greased
muffin rings placed on a lightly floured board. Leave to prove in a
warm place, covered with a damp cloth, for 45-50 minutes.

Heat a lightly greased griddle or hot plate to a moderate temperature
and cook the muffins on it, still in the rings, for 5-7 minutes on each
side. When one side is cooked, remove the ring before turning over.
Split open and serve either hot, or toasted when cold, spread with
margarine. Makes six muffins.

Note: The proving time varies according to temperature. When ready for cooking, the
surface of the muffins will retain the impression of a fingertip when lightly pressed.

Shortages meant the British custom of queueing became even more common than usual. Here, shoppers in 1945 wait patiently in Wood Green, London, on the pavement outside Williamsons bakers, not for bread but for cakes, as they hoped for a change from home-baked eggless, milkless, butterless "war cake".

< Favourite wartime brands like Twinings and Brooke Bond are still familiar to tea drinkers today, but others struggled to survive the war. Mazawattee tea, here in a gas-proof one-pound tin, became a major war casualty when its London factory was completely destroyed in 1940 bombing, though the brand has recently been relaunched.

> Everybody in the country had a ration book. Most were buff coloured but children under the age of 5 had books with green covers, as did pregnant women and recent mothers (who were allowed more milk, eggs, and fruit). Petrol ration books were also green, while clothing books were red. Young people aged 5 to 16 had blue books.

Due to the demanding nature of their work, canalboat workers were entitled to extra rations of tea and sugar, which they obtained using special vouchers. Here, boatman Ronald Hambridge picks up his rations from the Grand Union Canal HQ at Hayes in Middlesex.

In 1942 the Ministry of Food (MoF) invited 25 women to London to demonstrate how they made the most of rations. Mrs Lillie Taylor of Oldham was among them, reporting that she found a greater variety of supplies in London and shorter queues. She made the MoF custard, scones, and vegetable soup with savoury dumplings.

> The government encouraged people to boost their rations via a series of "Off the Ration" exhibitions at locations including Regent's Park Zoo, by keeping animals such as rabbits and pigs. This one featuring live chickens was held in the underground station at Charing Cross, supervised by Land Girls M. Slingsby and A. Chesterton.

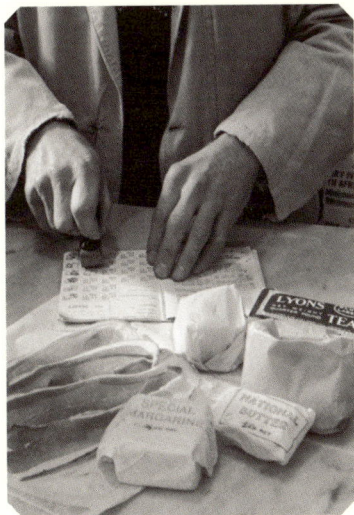

< Inside ration books were sets of coupons which the shopkeeper stamped as the provisions were provided. Here is the quarter pound of Lyons Blue Label tea – a blend of whole leaf grades which needed five minutes' infusion for the best flavour – allowance for a week, plus sugar, "National Butter", bacon, and "Special Margarine".

Along with tea and food, troops were issued with additional rations, particularly boiled sweets such as acid drops and barley sugars for energy. Checking the RAF store room rations at a depot in Uxbridge are members of the Women's Auxiliary Air Force.

Daisy Cook from Devon was one of many women who, instead of doing factory work, trained as signal box operators when signalmen were conscripted, often helping out as porter, booking clerk, and general dogsbody around train stations. Off duty, she picks up her rations with her young daughter at Bishop's Nympton's village shop in 1943.

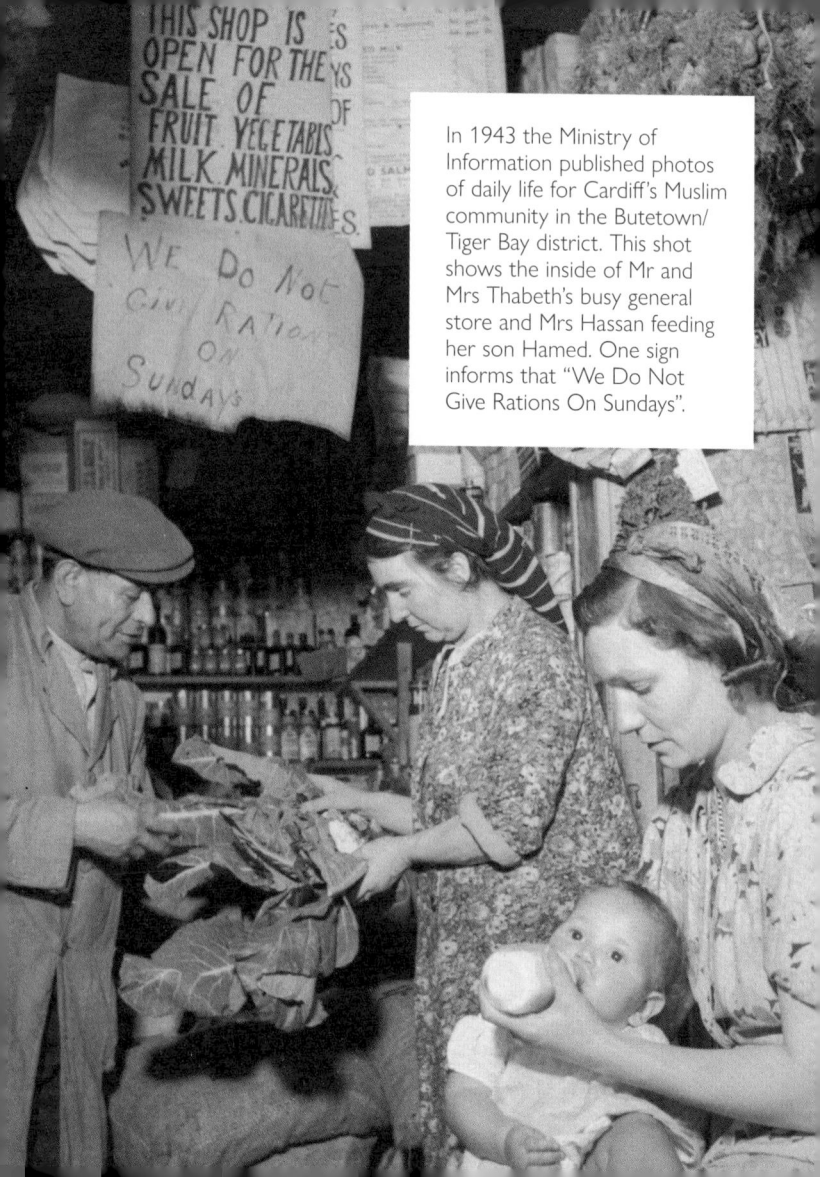

THIS SHOP IS
OPEN FOR THE
SALE OF
FRUIT VEGETABLES
MILK MINERALS.
SWEETS CIGARETTES.

WE DO NOT
GIVE RATION
ON
SUNDAYS

In 1943 the Ministry of Information published photos of daily life for Cardiff's Muslim community in the Butetown/Tiger Bay district. This shot shows the inside of Mr and Mrs Thabeth's busy general store and Mrs Hassan feeding her son Hamed. One sign informs that "We Do Not Give Rations On Sundays".

For many people, tea without milk was unthinkable. The weekly adult milk ration from November 1941 was two pints a week, supplemented by a tin of "Household Milk" powder which supposedly provided another four a month (though this was more suitable for cooking with than adding to a mug of tea…).

DON'T TOUCH
BLACK MARKET
GOODS...
KEEP PRICES DOWN
PUT YOUR MONEY INTO
5/- NATIONAL SAVINGS STAMPS

The black market offered a route for people willing to pay "spivs" or those shopkeepers who bent the rules for additional items like tea. It was risky though – courts had the power to impose £500 fines and by the end of the war, more than 100,000 prosecutions had been made related to black market goings-on.

One gripe about rations was regarding quantities. Aaron Gompertz, chair of the South Shields Food Control Committee, told the local newspaper he'd informed the Ministry of Food that tea was a "staple commodity" and 2oz a week was scarcely enough for "men working long shifts and having to take tea with them to their work".

BAKED JAM SPONGE

1½ tablespoons margarine or cooking fat
1½ tablespoons sugar
3 tablespoons finely grated raw carrot
6 tablespoons self-raising flour, or plain flour and
 ½ teaspoon baking powder
Milk
3-4 tablespoons jam
 (fresh fruit pulp will do just as well in summer time)

Cream together the fat and sugar. Beat in the carrot, then lightly add the flour. Moisten to a creamy consistency with milk, or milk and water.

Spread half the jam or fruit in the bottom of a greased pie dish, pour in the pudding mixture and spread it evenly. Bake in a moderate oven for 25 minutes. Just before serving, spread the rest of the jam or fruit on the top and put back in the oven for 3-4 minutes.

ENJOY IT WITH
A CUPPA

While tea was an essential ingredient in almost everybody's day during wartime, so were the little treats that went with it, such as toast, cakes, buns, and biscuits. Of course hostilities meant that some compromises had to be made. Ingredient shortages meant chocolate bars, a popular little luxury, had a different texture and taste. Similarly, the Ministry of Food encouraged people to eat rock cakes as these required less sugar and egg.

As an illustration of the impact of war, McVitie's produced 370 different varieties of cakes and biscuits in 1939, but just ten six years later. Their competitor Huntley & Palmers had the foresight to conserve samples of its 400 biscuit varieties in special individual tins to make sure they could be properly reproduced when peace finally returned.

Yet the changes enforced by rationing were no barrier to invention. Hugely popular food writer and broadcaster Ambrose Heath managed to knock out 29 recipe books during the war, including the likes of *Good Drinks*, *Making the Most of It*, and *The Good Cook in Wartime*. Generally, recipes often emphasised the importance of stretching what was available, typified by the Ministry of Food pamphlet entitled *Making the Most of Sugar*. Necessity being the mother of invention, beekeeping increased dramatically and honey often acted as a more than decent substitute for those with a sweet tooth.

War brought changes to the workplace. Although tea ladies providing hot cuppas in offices and factories were not unknown before the outbreak of hostilities, they increased substantially in numbers after 1939 and became a key part of the workforce around the country, helping to keep spirits up. People were also introduced to the delights of Spam and powdered egg, and (less successfully) tinned snoek fish and margarine. With the strong backing of the Women's Institute (WI), the Ministry of Agriculture also encouraged people to preserve food by bottling and canning. Less than 2 per cent of homes had a fridge by the end of the war.

Instant tea did not become popular. It was the British and other allied soldiers who suffered the brunt of "compo" tea (so named since it came in their "composite ration"). This concoction arrived in a tin as a dehydrated block containing tea, powdered milk, and sugar. It was sprinkled on hot water, then boiled. Just about acceptable when warm, it developed an unappetising scummy surface as it cooled down.

Celebrity chef Marguerite Patten was among the contributors to the BBC radio programme *Kitchen Front*, offering ration-friendly advice to cooks at home. Catering for the services was on a much larger scale – these 1940 Women's Auxiliary Air Force cooks on an RAF base display ingredients required for scones to feed a hundred men.

What appears at first sight to be an ordinary breakfast with tea and toast in Mrs Olive Day's sitting room at home in South Kensington is in fact a testament to her sang-froid, as the windows behind her have either been criss-crossed with tape – to prevent the glass from shattering during bombing – or replaced with wooden boards.

Wartime milk shortages forced Rowntree's to halt Smarties production and use dark chocolate for its KitKat (whose packaging was temporarily changed to blue). Unable to produce its usual Dairy Milk, Cadbury's alternative was "Ration Chocolate" which used dried skimmed milk powder instead of fresh milk, plus sugar, oat flour, and cocoa butter.

Freshly baked bread and buns, shown here aboard HMS Battler in December 1943, were popular accompaniments at teatime. Battler was an American-built Royal Navy escort carrier which at this time was deployed in what was then known as Bombay (now Mumbai). In a departure from usual messing arrangements, meals on the ship were served centrally, cafeteria style.

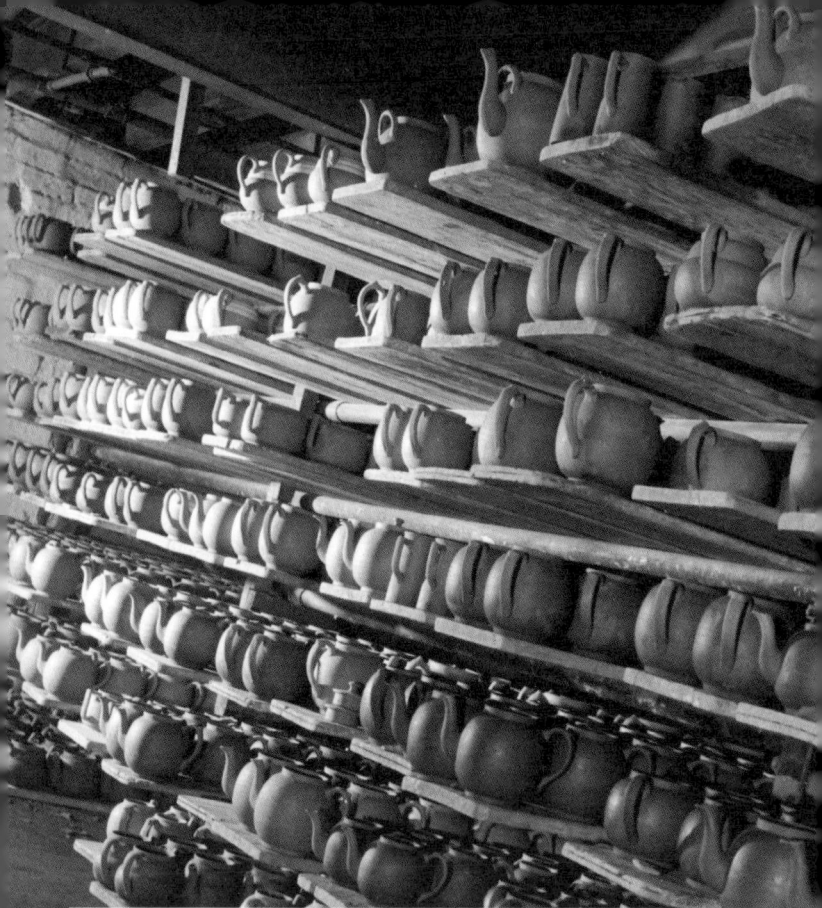

High tea consumption meant that high teapot production continued. One of the most prolific manufacturers was the longstanding J.G. Meakin, based in Stoke-on-Trent, which catered for both the domestic and international markets, especially British territories. These robust teapots are drying off on racks in the pottery in 1942.

Forming an orderly line in the well-stocked buffet car on this 1944 leave train between London and Scotland are soldiers of the Royal Engineers, looking forward to a few days' rest. To accompany the tea and Bovril is a range of cakes and sandwiches plus the welcome chance to buy chocolate without using ration coupons.

EGGLESS FRUIT CAKE

8oz self-raising flour
½ level teaspoon grated nutmeg
½ level teaspoon mixed spice
Pinch of salt
4oz margarine
4-6oz sultanas or currants
   (or mixed fruit)
2oz sugar
1 heaped tablespoon golden syrup
¼ pint hot water
½ level teaspoon bicarbonate of soda

Sieve the flour, nutmeg, spice, and salt together. Put the margarine, fruit, sugar, and syrup with the water in a saucepan, and bring to the boil. Allow to simmer for 3 minutes. Cool, and add the bicarbonate of soda.

Make a well in the centre of the flour, etc., pour in the cooled mixture and stir quickly together, mixing well.

Put into a 6-inch cake tin lined with greaseproof paper brushed with melted margarine, and bake for 1¼ hours on the middle shelf of a moderate oven. Cool on a wire tray.

In 1943 in rural North Yorkshire, two boys at the Catholic-run Ampleforth College enjoy tea and toast – made with a toasting fork – next to the fireplace in their study at school.

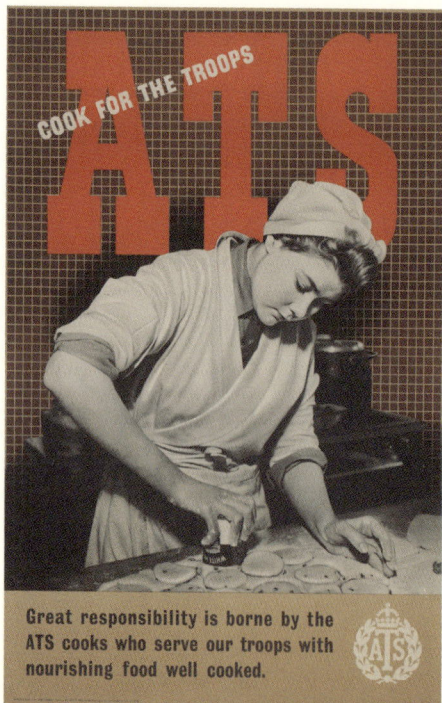

COOK FOR THE TROOPS

ATS

Great responsibility is borne by the ATS cooks who serve our troops with nourishing food well cooked.

Imagine tea without a biscuit! This recruitment poster to encourage women to join the Auxiliary Territorial Service (ATS) shows a recruit cutting out biscuit shapes from dough. Initially, ATS volunteers worked as cooks, clerks, orderlies, storewomen or drivers, but their role eventually expanded into all theatres of war. Princess Elizabeth added prestige to the ATS by joining in 1945.

Cigarettes, thought to help alleviate stress, were a staple of civilian and military life during the Second World War. They were not rationed, but priority was given to the troops, such as these men who are enjoying a smoke with a large pot of tea during a night watch on HMS Jackal.

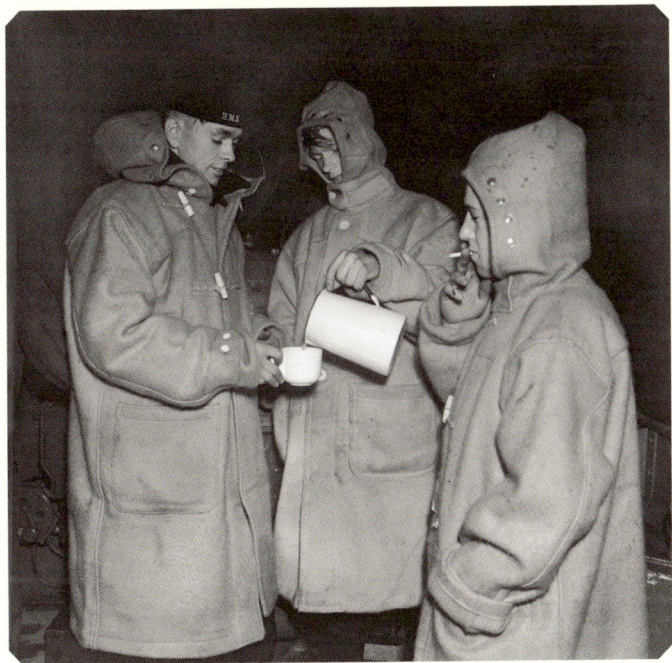

Tea and cake provided a useful way of welcoming the many people from other countries who took shelter in Britain during the hostilities. In April 1945 in Margate, Kent, Ms E. Grout serves tea to M. Tukuru, one of the 8,000 New Zealand prisoners of war who were rehabilitated in Britain.

GINGER BISCUITS

½ level teaspoon ground ginger
1 level teaspoon sugar
4oz self-raising flour
1½oz fat
1 tablespoon syrup

Mix the ginger and sugar with the flour, rub in the fat, mix in the syrup and knead until smooth. Make into a roll and cut into slices. This should make about a dozen biscuits.

Bake on a flat tin in a moderate oven for 15-20 minutes or until pale brown.

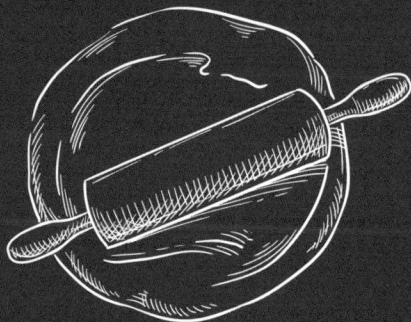

The Royal Army Service Corps established its first central School of Cookery at Aldershot in 1938, a recognition of the importance of cooks. Many instructors were civilian caterers. On a 1941 visit, Quartermaster-General to the Forces Sir Walter Venning watches a class of cooks making shortbread.

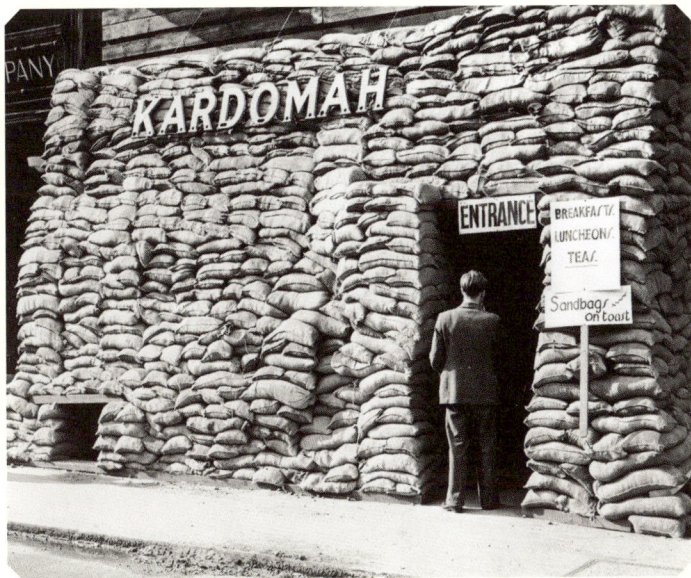

The Kardomah café chain had popular outlets across England, including this one on Fleet Street in London where novelist Barbara Pym was a regular and which, at the outset of the war in 1939, sandbagged itself as a publicity stunt. The sign outside offers "Breakfasts, Luncheons, Teas, Sandbags on toast".

The Dig for Victory campaign successfully encouraged people to grow their own food to boost their rations and counter the German U-boat blockade. Allotments were a key factor in this self-sufficiency, such as this one in Acton, Middlesex, where allotment holders have a rest with a tea and a sandwich in 1940.

The vicar's air-raid shelter

This cartoon by Heath Robinson is an example of war-era artwork that kept people laughing in the dark times. Others included David Low, who specialised in biting political satire, and Graham Laidler, known as "Pont", who gently poked fun at British quirks, such as their fondness for tea.

ON THE FRONT LINES

"The British soldier", wrote Field Marshal Sir Bernard Montgomery ("Monty") in his 1958 memoirs, "will do anything you ask of him so long as you arrange he gets his mail from home, the newspapers and, curiously enough, plenty of tea."

There were certainly plenty of opportunities for indulging. All bases had their own NAAFI (Navy, Army, Air Force Institutes) canteen – 7,000 were set up by 1944 – while mobile canteens run by a range of civilian organisations such as the YMCA provided sustenance when troops were on the move. Making tea was more problematic during a combat operation, but portable stoves were still available using mess tins or ration tins as makeshift kettles. A popular improvised solution in North Africa was known as a "Benghazi boiler", an empty fuel can which was partly filled with sand then doused in petrol and lit. Do not try this at home!

There were other obstacles too. In his 1992 account of serving in Burma (now officially and more commonly known as Myanmar) in 1945, *Quartered Safe Out Here*, novelist George MacDonald Fraser observed that: "Brewing up is not merely a matter of infusing tea; making the fire comes into it, and when you have lit and maintained fires in the monsoon, you have nothing more to learn."

This devotion to the elixir led to a myth that British soldiers even interrupted the heat of battle to get the kettle on. This was not helped by fictional examples of it in films such as *A Bridge Too Far*, and reports from an ambush in the French town of Villers-Bocage in 1944 when German tanks surprised the 22nd Armoured Brigade who were having a tea outside their tanks. The truth, of course, wasn't that they stopped to brew up, they brewed up because they had stopped – mugs of tea not only offered troops an energy boost and help with hydration, they also provided a calming pause and evoked happy memories of home. Also, tea masked the taste of water transported in cans previously used for distributing oil.

Tea helped other nations to keep calm and carry on, too. RAF bombers heading to Germany on nighttime raids in March 1941 took the time to "tea bomb" ten cities in the occupied Netherlands with 75,000 pouches of tea that had been sent to Britain from the Dutch East Indies. These 1oz bags were accompanied by a label saying "The Netherlands will rise again. ... Keep your spirits up". It was reported that the Dutch people were very grateful since it was almost impossible to get an ounce of tea in their shops.

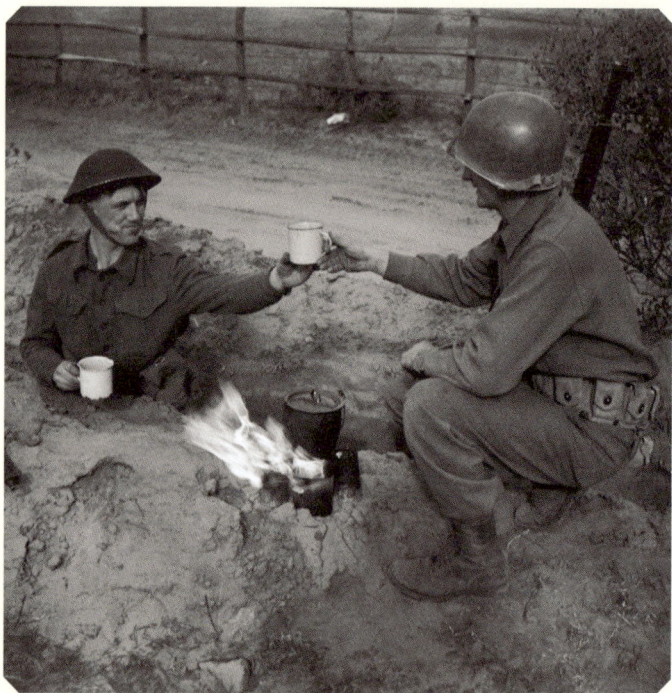

"The British don't know how to make a good cup of coffee," stated the 1942 *Instructions for American Servicemen in Britain* pamphlet, to which came the reply: "You don't know how to make a good cup of tea. It's an even swap." In 1944 at Anzio, Italy, a soldier from the 2/7th Middlesex Regiment and an American infantryman enjoy a tea.

Edward Ardizzone was one of 300 artists chosen by The War Artists Advisory Committee to chronicle the war. Nearly 6,000 works were completed by 1945. This example depicts a quiet moment in Sant'Arcangelo in Italy when British soldiers prepare the tea, watched by locals above.

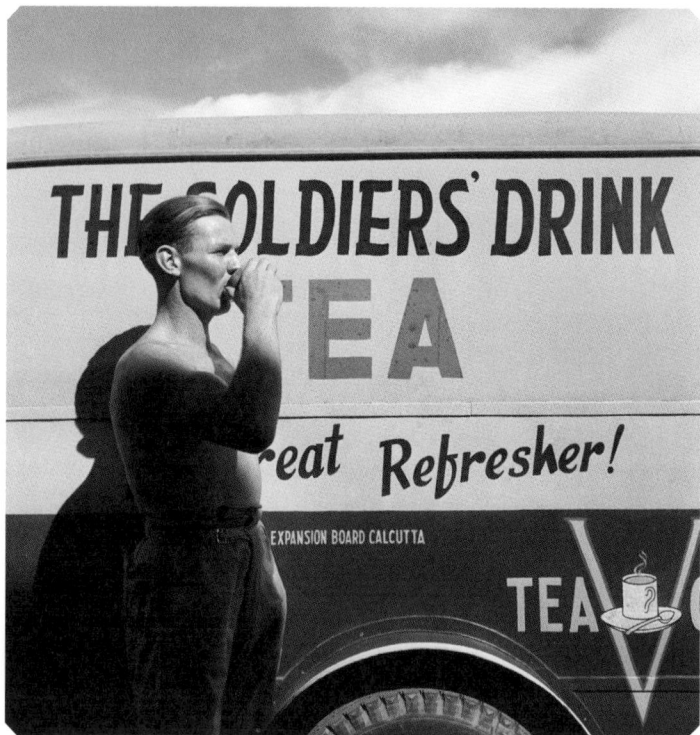

Cecil Beaton was best known as a fashion, and then royal, photographer, but in 1944 the Ministry of Information commissioned him to take photographs of the Allied war effort in various countries, including India. Among them is this shot of a soldier enjoying a tea by a Red Cross mobile tea wagon at Calcutta (now Kolkata) airport.

Even in the smallest of surroundings, tea was an essential. This soldier from the Royal Army Service Corps is lighting a cigarette in his tiny defensive dugout – known as a slit trench – while boiling water in a mess tin on an improvised stove made from a 25lb shell case.

Although the Navy's historic rum ration was still in operation (it ended in 1970), tea was still hugely popular in British submarines during the war. Stoker H. Shrubsole from Folkstone pours a cup in November 1944 for leading stoker W. Hughes from Liverpool on board HMS Seraph, a key player in the clandestine Operation Mincemeat.

Tea even entered the military vocabulary: when armoured vehicles caught fire, they were described as "brewing up". It was said you could tell if a Sherman tank had American or British crew if tea kettles were hanging off the turret. Here, a British crew in Burma (now Myanmar) have used their kettle to make tea during a break.

African soldiers formed a major part of the Allied fighting force – 90,000 from East and West Africa fought in Burma (now Myanmar) alone. These men are taking a break from training duties in Ceylon (now Sri Lanka) to enjoy a cup of the country's fine, high-quality tea, a staple of the domestic British market.

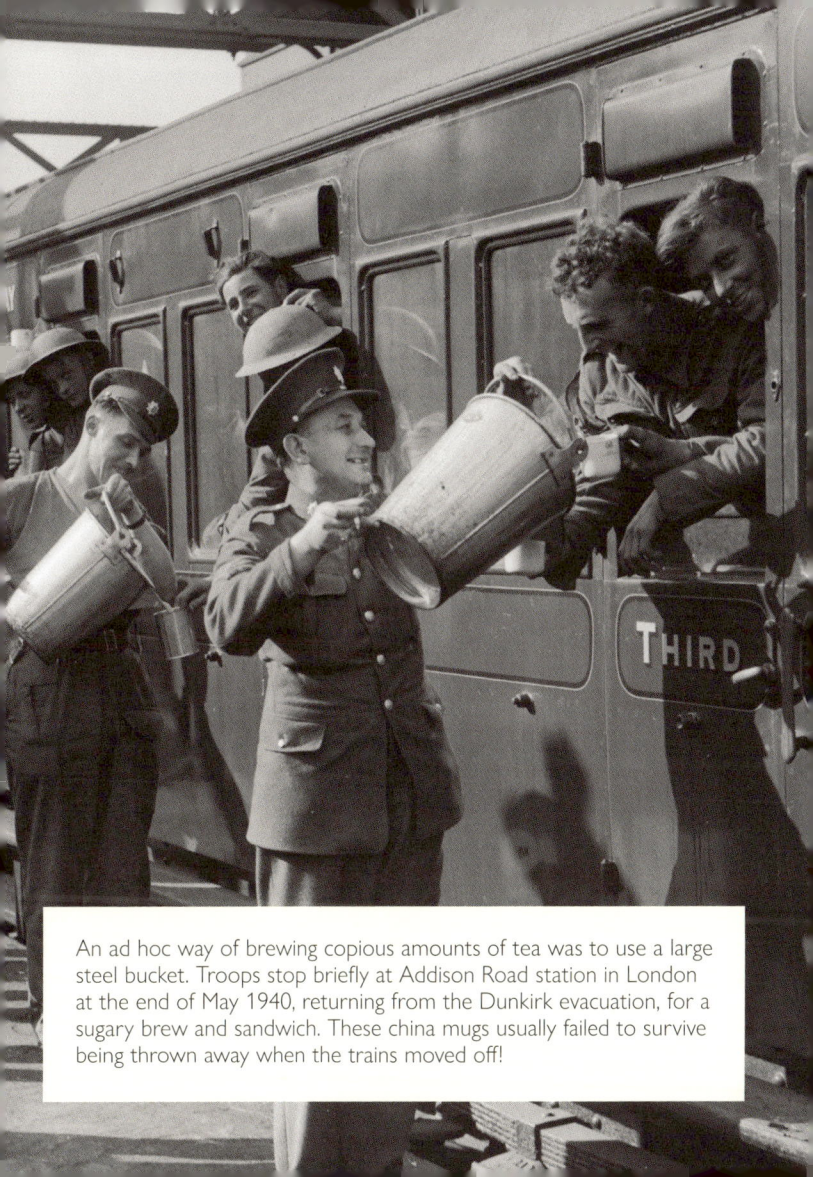

An ad hoc way of brewing copious amounts of tea was to use a large steel bucket. Troops stop briefly at Addison Road station in London at the end of May 1940, returning from the Dunkirk evacuation, for a sugary brew and sandwich. These china mugs usually failed to survive being thrown away when the trains moved off!

Set up in 1939, the Entertainments National Service Association (better known as ENSA) delivered entertainment – of varying quality – to the armed forces. Gracie Fields performed for the British Expeditionary Force in France in 1940 and dispensed tea to them (and unexplained monkeys!) in a village near Valenciennes.

The Short Sunderland was a long-range flying boat used for anti-submarine reconnaissance patrols. It could stay in the air for up to 18 hours which meant its galley and kerosene stove were vital in feeding and watering the crew of up to ten. A gunner turns chef to make tea.

These soldiers enjoy a comforting cup of tea on December 25, 1944, next to their modest but still very much valued Christmas tree. The photo was taken by leading war photographer Bert Hardy of the Army Film and Photographic Unit, a regular contributor to the hugely successful *Picture Post* magazine.

Job done, time for a tea for British soldiers at the Brandenburg Gate in Berlin at a NAAFI (Navy, Army, Air Force Institutes)/ EFI (Expeditionary Force Institutes) mobile canteen, almost certainly the first of its kind in the German capital, on July 16, 1945. Five days later, there was a British parade through the city to celebrate victory.

Together, the British Red Cross and Order of St John sent 20 million food parcels to prisoners of war, saving many lives in the process thanks to the extra nourishment they provided. These typically included tins of food (used to brew tea when emptied), chocolate, dried milk, Marmite, processed cheese, and of course, tea.

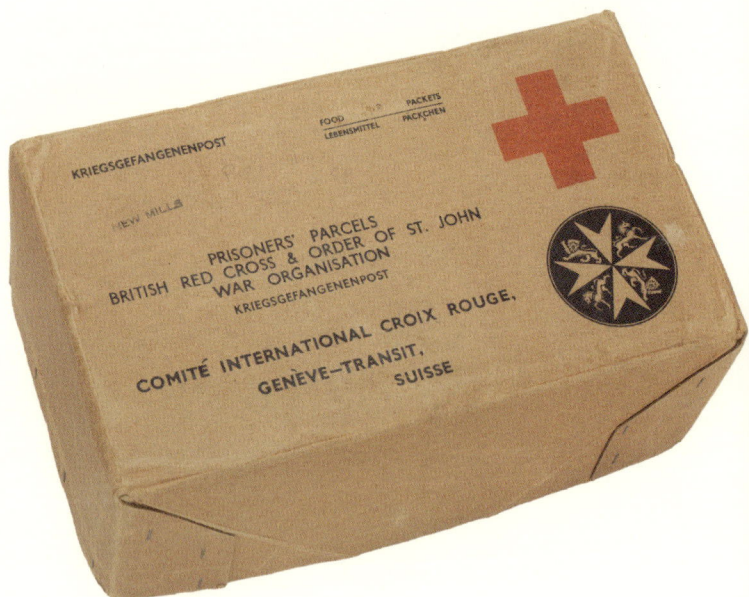

One of the biggest problems in the Western Desert campaigns in Egypt and Libya was simply keeping food and drink clean and fit for consumption. The British officer here is using salvaged enemy gas mask containers to store necessities such as tea and sugar against the relentless intrusion of sand.

THE HOME FRONT

Tea was a comforting part of daily wartime home life, whether savoured in the kitchen or the Anderson shelter, during tea parties organised by WI members for evacuees, or at the end of the war at VE Day parties.

It's no exaggeration to say that tea was as important to the war effort at home as the weaponry for the military on the front line. Prime Minister Winston Churchill was fully aware of its symbolic importance in terms of keeping up morale, and is said to have described tea as more powerful than ammunition (he himself preferred whisky and soda at teatime). A familiar and classless comfort for millions, it's easy to see why hot, sweet tea was often handed out in the aftermath of bombing raids.

The humble teapot reflected this positive fighting spirit. Preston-based catalogue club company Dyson and Horsfall usually gave an aluminium teapot to its regional agents as a festive gift. But when the metal became crucial to armament production, they gave pottery teapots instead, featuring the British and French flags, other flags from the colonies, and the words "WAR AGAINST HITLERISM", "RIGHT SHALL PREVAIL", and "LIBERTY AND FREEDOM" on the sides. One turned up on the BBC's *Antiques Roadshow* in 2019.

Churchill also arranged for black-glazed Staffordshire ceramic teapots, emblazoned with the handpainted motto "FOR U.S.A. BRITAIN AND DEMOCRACY" to be sent to America to encourage its involvement in the war, as well as raise funds and help pay for transatlantic convoy costs.

Tea was crucial for keeping workers' spirits up. A 1941 wartime booklet produced by the Empire Tea Bureau, called *Tea for the Workers: How to Make the Best of the Factory Tea Ration,* included this comment from the production manager of a large munition works: "We wanted the works to have its tea; we knew production and morale benefitted. Tea had to be supplied or there would have been a grievance."

Catering on an industrial scale was certainly no mean feat – the booklet lists various ways of getting tea to the workers, including roving tea trolleys within a factory, tea cars/mobile canteens on sites outdoors, static tea bars at fixed points within buildings, and of course tea served in canteens. It also looked at the economics of bulk tea-making and timings for an efficient trolley service, as well as warning managers to look out for those bringing their own pint-sized mugs to work hoping for a cheeky top-up.

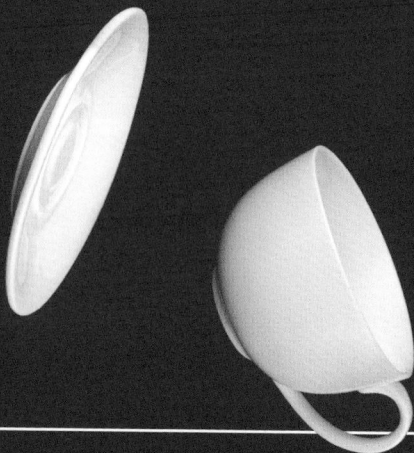

There was certainly tea-based mischief at Bletchley Park in Buckinghamshire, the hush- hush home of the code-breakers who did so much to win the war while still on home turf. Although there was an official tea room, staff often took their tea and went for a wander and a ponder around the estate's large ornamental lake. But rather than return the tea cups and saucers to the canteen, staff frequently simply lobbed them into the lake, until crockery losses became so great, tea drinkers were made to provide their own. Leading cryptologist Alan Turing took further steps to prevent colleagues pinching his mug, leaving it chained to a radiator when not in use.

Supplies were short, rather than strictly rationed, in the nation's tea shops. Perhaps the best known of these were the Lyons Corner Houses, among them the Coventry Street premises. A 1941-2 menu from the nearby Oxford Street outlet indicates that tea could be had at 3d per cup or 4d per pot (per person).

CARROT CAKE

3oz fat
6oz flour
1 level teaspoon baking powder
3oz oatmeal
1½ tablespoons sugar
1 tablespoon dried fruit
3 tablespoons grated raw carrot
1 dessertspoon syrup
1 dried egg (reconstituted)
Water

Rub the fat into the flour, add the dry ingredients and carrots and mix thoroughly. Add the syrup, reconstituted egg, and sufficient water to form a fairly stiff consistency.

Place in a greased tin and bake in a moderate oven for 1 hour.

Despite bombings, theatres did their best to stay open. These women were among those enjoying not only the performance but also a cup of tea (china, of course, and served to them in their seats) during the interval of the opera *La Traviata* at the New Theatre, St Martin's Lane in 1943.

∧ While King George VI and Queen Elizabeth – here visiting the Admiralty canteen during tea break – were taking tea in Buckingham Palace on September 13, 1940, it was hit by five bombs. "I am glad we have been bombed," said Queen Elizabeth. "It makes me feel I can look the East End in the face."

∧ It wasn't only young children who were evacuated from England's capital to the provinces. These students from King's College London enjoying a cup of tea in a Bristol café were among many from London's universities who found refuge around the country in Swansea, Oxford, Nottingham, and Cambridge.

Tea was needed at all times of the day. Patience "Boo" Brand and Rachel Bingham were society girls in 1941 who were also members of the hardworking Women's Voluntary Service, rising as early as 2.30am to begin filling large Thermos urns with tea to distribute to those lodged overnight in trench shelters.

∧ Air raid shelters came in all shapes and sizes. These street surface shelters in Stoke Newington, London, were built in brick and concrete, and featured bunk beds as well as everything needed for making tea. However, there were quality control issues and these shelters never proved popular.

＞ Many contemporary accounts describe the solace that a hot cup of tea provided to those who suffered. In 1944, PC Frederick Godwin of Gipsy Hill Police Station was on hand to offer comfort to this man after his wife was killed by the bomb that destroyed their home while he was out walking the dog.

A Y.M.C.A. TEA CAR SERVES AN A.A. GUN UNIT

There was much pride in being part of the mobile canteen service. Miss R. C. Desch describes in her personal journal how she felt "fortunate enough" to be picked as a driver for a YMCA canteen van providing sustenance to demolition and rescue squads as well as those who had been bombed out.

BROWN BREAD

3½ teaspoons salt
3½lb flour
1oz yeast
1 teaspoon caster sugar
1½ pints tepid water

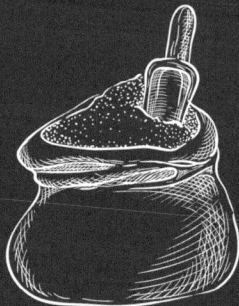

Mix the salt and flour, and place in a warm basin in a hot place to heat slightly.

Cream the yeast and sugar together in a slightly warmed basin. The mixture should become liquid. Add the tepid water, which should be just the temperature of your little finger. Make a well in the centre of the warm flour, pour in the liquid and sprinkle a little flour over it. This accelerates the growth of the yeast.

Cover the basin with a warm cloth and put to rise in a warm place for 20 minutes. Then mix the contents of the bowl and knead until the dough is smooth and elastic. Put into a floured bowl and leave it covered in a warm place until it doubles in size.

Knead again. Divide the dough into four 1lb loaves. Put them in a warm place until the required size is reached. Bake in a hot oven until the loaf is golden brown and sounds hollow if tapped underneath. Cooking time is about ¾-1 hour for a 1lb loaf.

Wartime Home Secretary Herbert Morrison (a keen dancer) was applauded when he announced in 1942 that dancing did not hinder the war effort so would not be prohibited. Tea dances like this one in Bournemouth, often organised by the Red Cross or local churches, provided sociable relief for both soldiers and civilians.

During the war, people were strongly encouraged to avoid non-essential travel and "Holiday at Home" – the government even cancelled the 1940 August Bank Holiday. Among those doing their patriotic bit in 1943 in the back garden were Peggy Franks (pouring tea) and her chum Pinkie Barnes.

If you had no outside space for a corrugated Anderson shelter, you could try an indoor Morrison shelter, built from a self-assembly kit. Because of its sturdy steel top, it could also double up as a dining table! Both types of shelter were free to householders with low incomes.

CRUMPETS

¾oz yeast or ¾oz dried yeast
1 level teaspoon sugar
1 pint lukewarm water
1lb 2oz plain flour
½ level teaspoon bicarbonate of soda
¼ pint cold water
5 level teaspoons salt

Blend the yeast with the sugar, and gradually stir in the lukewarm water. Sieve the flour, make a hole in the centre, pour in the yeast mixture, stir together until thoroughly mixed, cover, and leave in a warm place for 1½ hours. Blend the bicarbonate of soda smoothly with the ¼ pint of cold water. Add to the yeast and flour mixture, beating well. Leave to stand for 10 minutes longer in a warm place. Finally stir in the salt.

Grease the crumpet rings lightly, and place on a moderately hot, non-greased griddle or hot plate. Ladle the batter into the rings, allowing about ⅛ of a pint (or 5 tablespoons) for each, and cook over a moderate heat until the surface is well covered with holes (8-10 minutes). Then remove the rings, turn and cook the other side. Serve hot, spread with margarine, or toast when cold, and spread with margarine. Makes 18 crumpets.

The Women's Voluntary Services for Air Raid Precautions (WVS) was established in 1938 to provide food and drink plus first aid help before and after air raids – this WVS van is dishing out tea and buns to men clearing up after an attack on London. By 1943, the WVS had a million volunteers working in many home front activities.

> Eileen Barry, Audrey Willis, Betty Long and Audrey Prickett enjoying tea on a Sussex farm with the farmer after rat-catching. They were among thousands of women who signed up to the Women's Land Army to replace conscripted male farm workers. In 1939, their weekly wages were 28 shillings (about £1.40) for a 50-hour week.

∧ In this basement shelter in 1940, members of the Air Raid Precautions (ARP), who helped to protect civilians from air raids, enjoy tea and treats served by a young lad. The "SP" on his helmet indicates he belonged to a Stretcher Party, which helped extricate casualties from bombed buildings.

THE BREW THAT
GOT US THROUGH

The Second World War saw tea's finest hour. It was the background to daily life, a balm in trying times, and the embodiment of the determined British spirit, a kind of liquid cricket. In August 1939, the painter Eric Ravilious produced his iconic watercolour *Tea at Furlongs*, a rural evocation of Britain just before the storm. In 1945, poet Sir John Betjeman wrote lovingly of a couple meeting *In A Bath Teashop*. These bookends suggest that even a global war could not alter the unwavering place of tea at centre stage in British life.

As this book shows, images of tea in photographs, on posters, in art — making it, drinking it, offering it to others — became synonymous with ideas of bravery and seeing it through together. Don't panic — they suggest — keep calm and make tea.

One of the beauties of tea during the Second World War was that it was for everybody, from Wrens flying transport planes to Bevin Boys mining for coal. The "Tea Revives You" poster campaign run by the Empire Marketing Board at the time promoted this universal appeal of the drink. The jolly Disneyesque character "Mr T. Pott" also made frequent appearances in adverts, on both sides of the Atlantic, suggesting that "Tea Drives Away the Droops" and "Anytime is Tea Time".

The war also cemented the place of the tea trolley and works canteen in the British workplace, the numbers of canteens roughly doubling between 1939 and 1945 as employers looked to keep workers healthy and happy (not to mention, productive). Factory canteens were particlarly uncommon before the war, for example, in cotton mills, but were a very welcome addition to those working long hours in difficult conditions.

Since the end of the war we've seen the rise of the tea bag, the growing impact of instant coffee (thanks not least to US servicemen stationed in Britain during wartime), and a flood of fizzy drinks. But tea has by no means gone the way of the dodo. We still drink more than a hundred million cups of tea a day and the UK Tea & Infusions Association reports that more than three quarters of people find out what's happening in the office via a cup of tea rather than by any other way. There's even an annual National Tea Day on April 21.

This 1939 poster from the Empire Marketing Board – set up a decade earlier to encourage people to buy goods from Britain's colonies – emphasised that tea was the kind of modern, wholesome, uplifting drink that could be enjoyed by anybody and at any time. The series stressed that tea was for women as well as men.

Tea was an ever-present prop in British films made during the war. It's especially to the fore in the very British 1945 romantic drama *Brief Encounter*, with significant scenes taking place in a railway station refreshment room.

This tea cup and mug were made specially for two of the numerous street party celebrations in south London to mark VE Day on May 8, 1945. Both were given to children at the time, the tea cup – featuring portraits of Stalin, Churchill and Roosevelt – at a knees-up in Camberwell. The mug, with its simple design, also survived the festivities.

MENU
FOR
STAFF OF 92 BRITISH GENERAL HOSPITAL
on
V·E DAY

BREAKFAST – 07-00 HOURS
PORRIDGE
FRIED EGG, BACON, FRIED BREAD
MARMALADE, BREAD
AND BUTTER, TEA.

LUNCH – 13-00 HOURS
COLD MEATS
LETTUCE, RADISH, FENNEL, SPRING
ONION SALAD, MAYONNAISE SAUCE,
FRUIT FLAN & CREAM

TEA – 16-00 HOURS
FRUIT SALAD & CREAM,
TRUMAN TRIFLE. BREAD & BUTTER
CHURCHILL CAKE, TEA.

DINNER – 18-00 HOURS
ROAST PORK, SAGE & ONION STUFFING
APPLE SAUCE, ROAST & CREAMED POTATOES,
PEAS, VICTORY PUDDING & BRANDY SAUCE.
CHEESE & BISCUITS
ASSORTED NUTS, FRUIT.
CIGARETTES & BEER
RUNNING BUFFET IN THE "SMUGGLERS' REST" FROM 21-00 HOURS

VE Day was celebrated all around the world. Here is the staff menu for the celebrations that took place at 92nd British General Hospital in Naples. Tea is in evidence, from the slap-up breakfast through to 4pm teatime, before being replaced for dinner with beer.

Necessity was the mother of invention for many people who had trouble accessing tea easily. This teapot was made for British civilian prisoner of war Eric Forrester at a camp in the Ardèche, France, by a friendly Polish internee who used empty powdered milk cans to ensure Eric could make best use of the Red Cross food parcels.

Here's another example of never-say-die tea production under trying conditions. It was used by a Miss E. McIntyre, who had dual British and Dutch citizenship, at Liebenau civilian internment camp in Germany. She replaced the teapot's broken handle and lid with lots of wire and string, glue being unavailable.

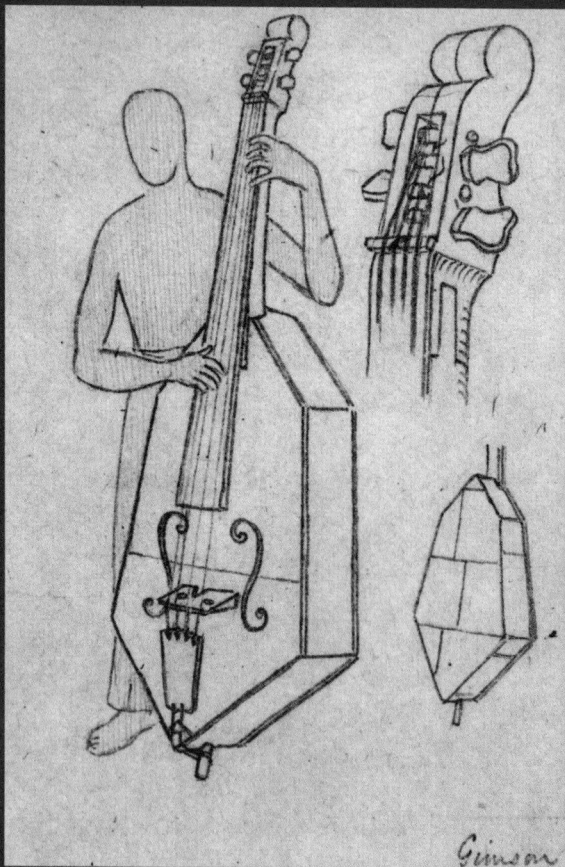

Gimson

N.A.A.F.I. MENU

SPAM
JAMBON
Petits Pâtés Viande
TORTES aux PRUNES
TARTES aux POMMES
Pommes frites
Café au lait
Thé

∧ Members of the Royal Air Force (RAF) and the French Air Force worked side by side in training, in the air, and in preparing the day's Navy, Army and Air Force Institutes (NAAFI) offerings. Here, French-speaking Miss Marjorie Austin from Guernsey puts together a menu with a French corporal, making sure there is plenty of *thé* as well as *café au lait*.

< Tea got people through in myriad ways. This sketch by Stanley Gimson shows an improvised double bass made using tea chests in Chungkai camp. Gimson was one of the finest chroniclers of the Japanese prisoner of war camps on the Burma–Siam railway.

∧ One of the most popular BBC radio programmes during the war was *Workers' Playtime*, a variety show with plenty of music and humour. It was broadcast live from British factory canteens three times a week, to raise spirits. Here, 1945 cotton workers in Lancashire make good use of their canteen's refreshment trolley (no ration books required).

❯ Cyril Bird, who signed himself Fougasse, was a journalist and cartoonist probably best known for his "Careless talk costs lives" posters which he produced without charge for the Ministry of Information. Here, in his usual mix of humour and caution, two leisurely tea drinkers are rather forcefully reminded to get on with their wartime repair jobs.

Merely to remind you that . . . .

TIME FLIES

(and especially where urgent repair jobs are concerned)

Two members of the Home Guard prepare tea in a hut in this painting by English artist Michael Ford. The civilian militia comprised around 1.5 million volunteers by July 1940 (including Ford himself), and was later immortalised – though rather inaccurately – in the popular television comedy series *Dad's Army*.

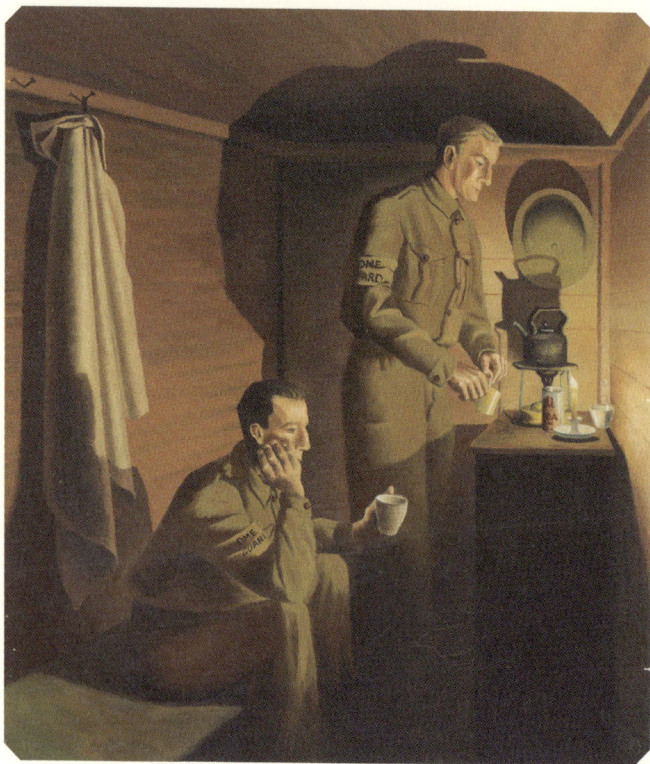

Established during the interwar years, the NAAFI really came of age in the Second World War, offering food, drink, and other goods to the armed forces – it is still going strong today. Unofficial war artist James Boswell depicts soldiers making music and drinking tea in the NAAFI at the Royal Army Medical Corps depot in Crookham, Hampshire.

The durable enamel pint mug was issued to forces during the First World War, though was usually white with a blue rim. Towards the end of the Second World War a brown, similarly unmarked version was produced. It had three dots on the underside from when it rested on a tripod during the enamelling process.

A whole new generation of tea drinkers was born and grew up during the war. Here at Marchant's Hill School in Hindhead, Surrey – for children evacuated from London (now a PGL holiday camp) – June Beale, whose father was a Chief Petty Office in the Royal Navy, pours tea for her friends.

INDEX

Acknowledgements

Many thanks to Phyllis and Philip Johnson for providing me with access to their collection of books about tea and to Harley Griffiths and Sarah Woods at HarperCollins for all their help in putting it together.

Image Credits

(t) top; (b) bottom

Imperial War Museums

P11 H39254; P16 D7958; P18-19 D25034; P20 (t) EPH405; P20 (b) LBYK.10/339; P21 D21751; P22 V122; P23 (t) D7958; P23 (b) D2373; P24 D22223; P25 D1745I; P26 D152; P27 V114; P28 Art PST; P30 DB0179; P36 CH6747; P37 D2358; P38 EPH0283; P39 A21628; P40 D11463; P41 D18774; P43 D17357; P44 Art PST14532; P45 A348; P46 D24531; P48 H7798; P49 HU36138; P50-51 D477; P58 NA11770; P59 Art LD4801; P60 IB1882; P61 B13213; P62 A26381; P63 SE3335; P64 IND2438; P65 H1630; P66 F4072; P67 CH11085; P68 B13091; P69 BU8974; P70 EPH88; P71 E10291; P77 D6573; P79 D17188; P80 (t) A22625; P80 (b) D432; P81 D2154; P82 HU94177; P83 D17188; P84 Documents 179 © Rights Holder; P86 D16671; P87 D16038; P88 QHS102; P90 D2169; P91 (t) D11258; P91 (b) D1623; P98 (t) EPH4372; P98 (b) EPH4886; P99 Documents 10113; P100 EPH0127; P101 EPH720A; P102 HU3105; P103 CH138410; P104 D26007; P105 Art PST3703; P106 Art LD846; P107 Art LD1927; P108 EQU4311; P109 D21623.

Alamy

P52 Chronicle / Alamy Stock Photo; P96 Lordprice Collection / Alamy Stock Photo

Shutterstock

P5 Prokhorovich / Shutterstock; P76 Alexa Mat / Shutterstock; P97 ITV / Shutterstock; Recipes P17, P31, P42, P47, P78, P89 Qualit Design / Shutterstock; P84 Qualit Design / Shutterstock

Recipe Credits

Recipes on pages 17, 31, 42, 47, 78, 85 and 89 were previously published in *Victory in the Kitchen: Wartime Recipes* (Imperial War Museums, 2016).